ULTRA 3-D Magic®

FINE ART PRINT BOOK

Front Line Art Publishing
Montage Publications Division
San Diego, California
•
Quarto Publishing
London, England

 Printed in China
 For information, write Montage Publications, 9808 Waples Street, San Diego, California 92121.

ISBN: I-56714-050-5

First Printing,

ULTRA 3-D Magic®

FOREWARD

Welcome to ULTRA 3-D MAGIC®, a new and challenging edition in the ULTRA 3D® series. Although 3-D images and stereograms have been around for decades in many different forms, we have now entered the age where we need only our eyes and minds to create amazing illusions of depth. This new art form is so visually stimulating, you will find yourself actually reaching out to touch the images that seem so real just beyond the printed page.

From the very first page of ULTRA 3-D MAGIC®, you realize that you are in for a fantastic ride. Through a wonderous mix of art and science, these amazing images will transport you to 26 different worlds, each with incredible detail and depth. As you stare at the fields of colors, lines and patterns, they will begin to swirl, move and separate when suddenly...

You are hunting with a wild pack of white wolves through snow capped mountains.

You are discovering the secrets of a mysterious cave and awaken the sleeping bats inside.

You are roaming the hills of a beautiful green countryside as the noble stallion leaps free of its gates.

You are climbing the wall of a great canyon when you by chance spy the mighty rams guarding the rocky cliffs.

Ultra 3-D MAGIC® has been created for everyone. An innovative and creative challenge to the most sophisticated viewer, and a relaxing experience for those who wish to enjoy a unique, new art form.

Enjoy

ULTRA 3-D MAGIC® art by Johnny Ray Barnes Jr. & Marty Engle
Cover design by Johnny Ray Barnes Jr. & Marty Engle

ULTRA 3-D Magic®

When viewed properly, Stereograms and 3-D art prints can spring to mind many pleasant surprises. Remember to relax (both the mind and eye) and have patience. There are several ways to view the prints depending on size and format:

GENERAL VIEWING INSTRUCTIONS:

View at eye level. Stand at a medium distance from the image (2 to 4 ft.). Concentrate on your reflection or the reflection of light on the image. Stare THROUGH the picture as if you were looking at something a distance BEHIND the image. Keep focused on one area of the image. Depending on eyesight of the viewer, different lengths of time may be required for the image to become clear. CONTINUE STARING as the image will appear. When the pattern begins to move or shift the image is about to form. If you have trouble seeing the image, try standing with your nose just touching the print. Stare at the print at this distance and keep your eyes fixed at that position while slowly backing away from the print. Continue backing away until the image begins to form. Be patient as it takes some practice.

IF THE PRINT IS BEHIND GLASS:

- Start by looking at your own reflection in the glass cover.
- Then look beyond the reflection into the back of the picture, as if you are looking through a window.
- Keep staring through the picture. Once you see the image the first time, it becomes easier to see it again.

IF THE PRINT HAS NO REFLECTIVE SURFACE:

- Hold the print just at the end of your nose. Let your eyes relax and let the picture be out of focus. Just keep staring through the picture, not at it.
- Slowly move the print away from your face, continuing to look through the picture. Stop at a comfortable reading distance.
- When you start to see an image come into focus, keep staring through it.

AN ALTERNATIVE TECHNIQUE:

- Focus on an object in the distance.
- Maintaining that focal point, insert the print between your eyes and the distant object.
- The print will be blurry, but that's OK. Keep your eyes focused exactly as they are, staring blankly, without actually "looking" at anything.
- Move the print slowly forward and backward.
- When the print reaches the right position, the three-dimensional image will come into focus.

JUNGLE KING

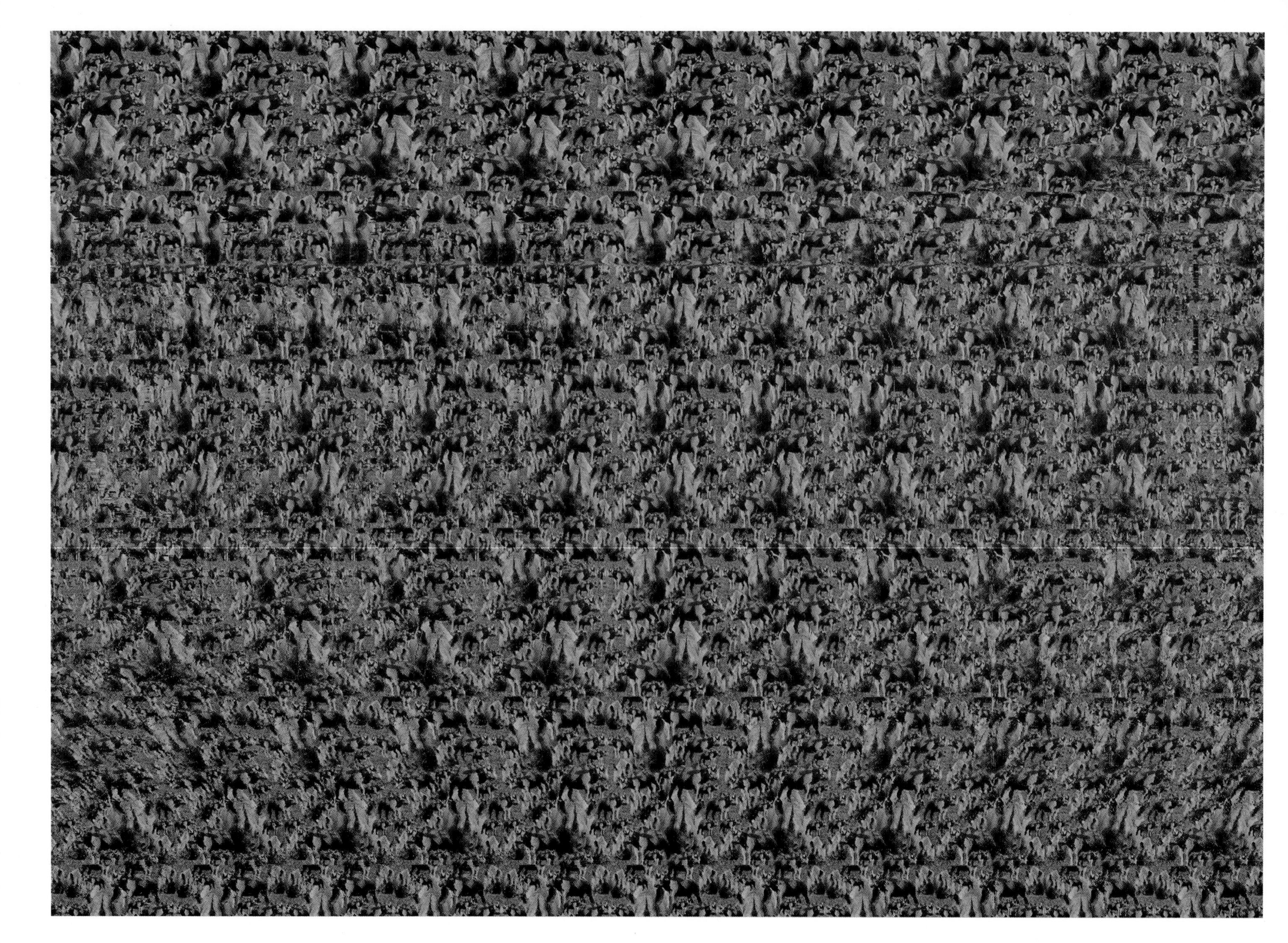

CHARGE!!

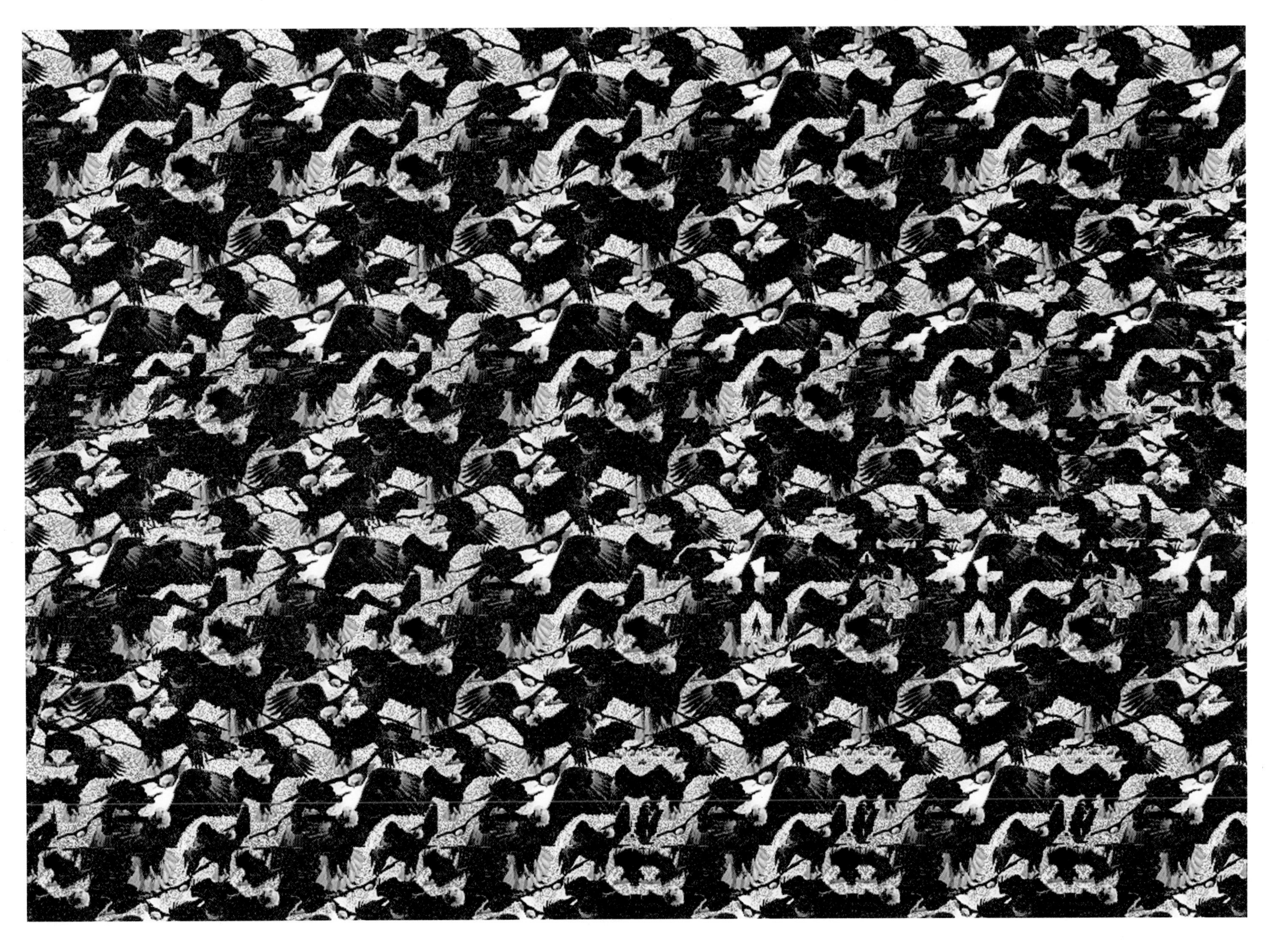

FLYING HOME

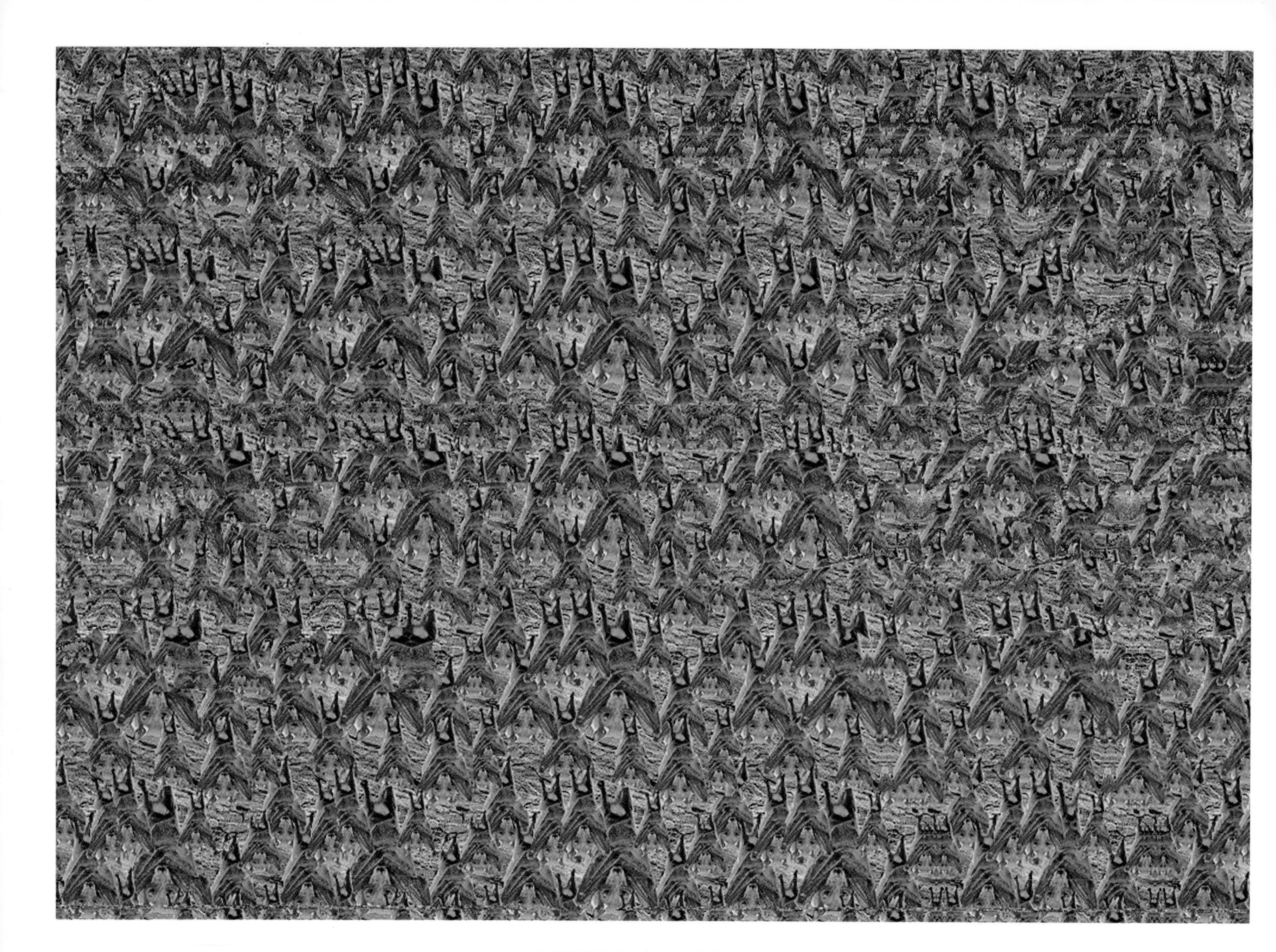

THE BAT CAVE

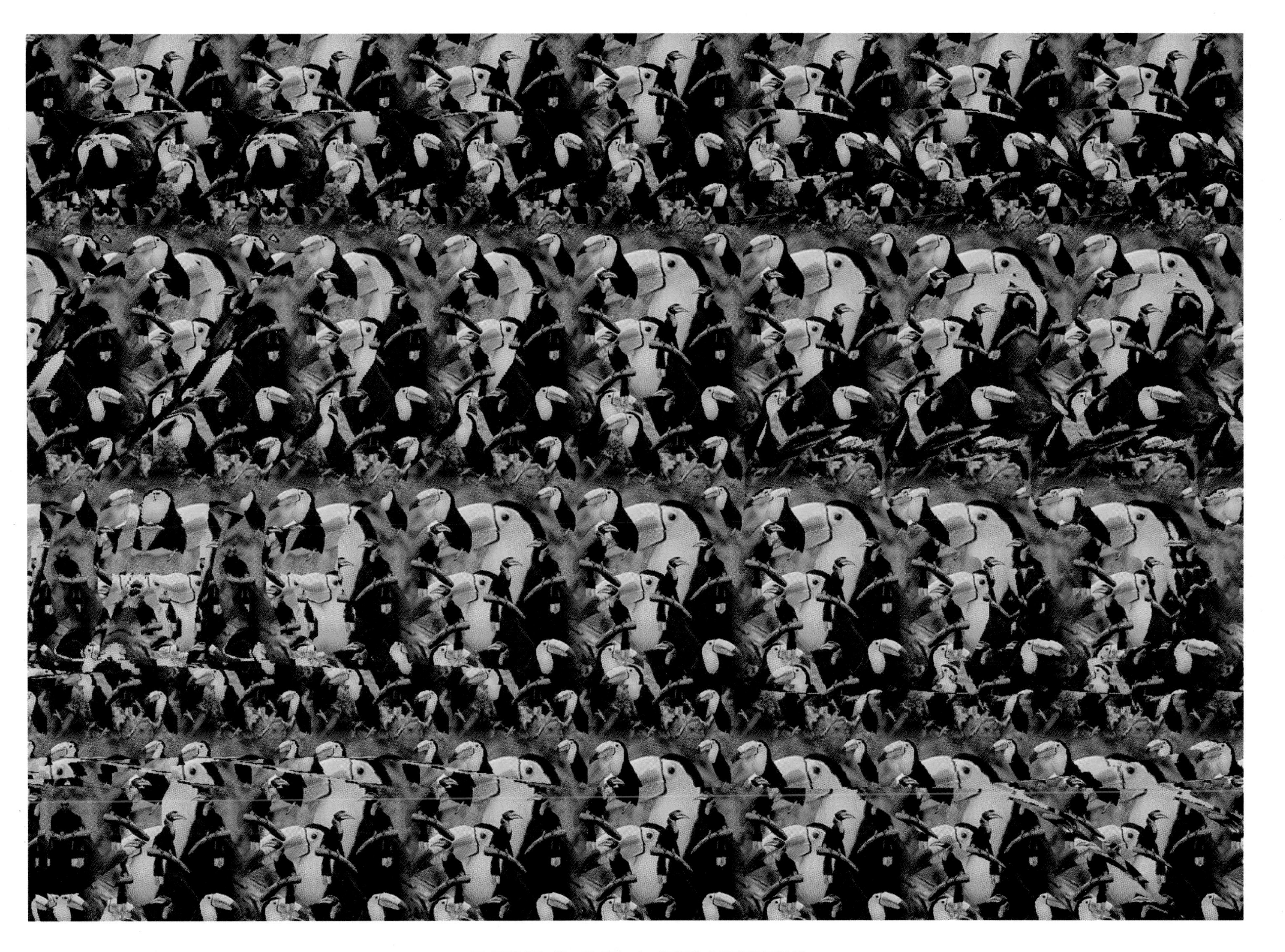

BIRDS OF A FEATHER

JUMPING THE GATE

NUTTY PALS

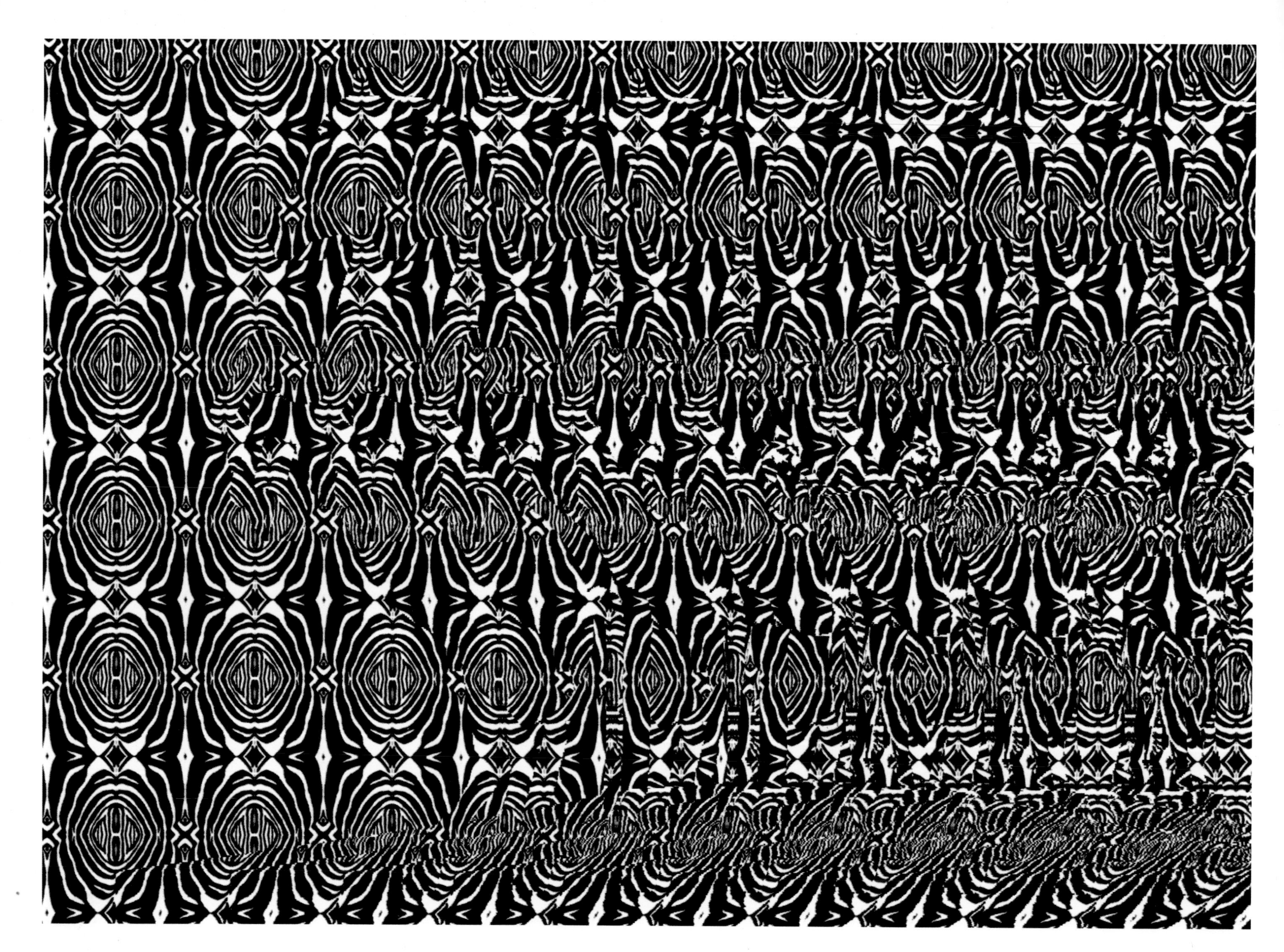

ZEBRA COUNTRY

ELEPHANTS

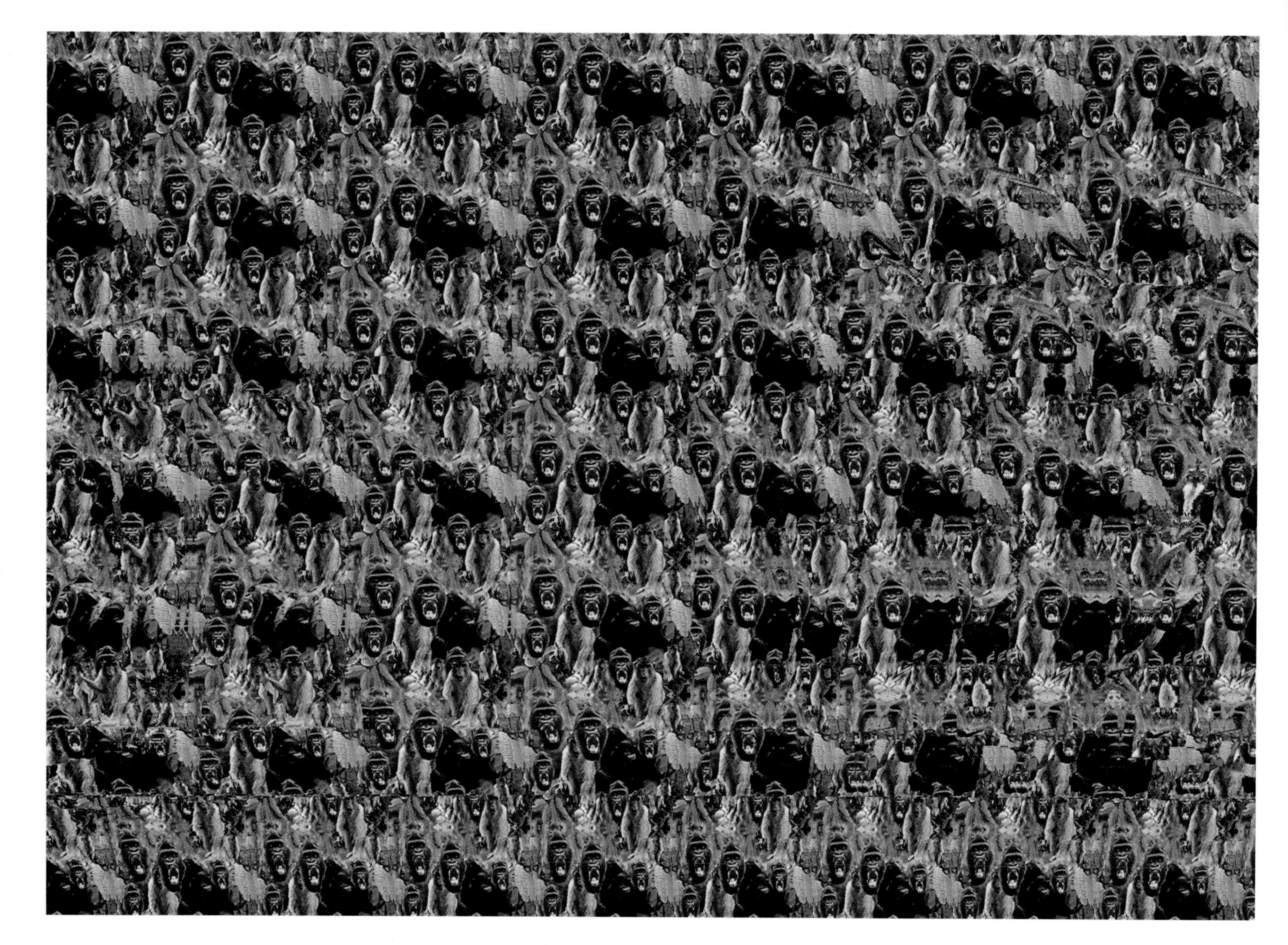

MONKEYING AROUND

MASTERS OF THE MOUNTAINTOPS

RABBIT SEASON

LAIR OF THE WHITE WOLF

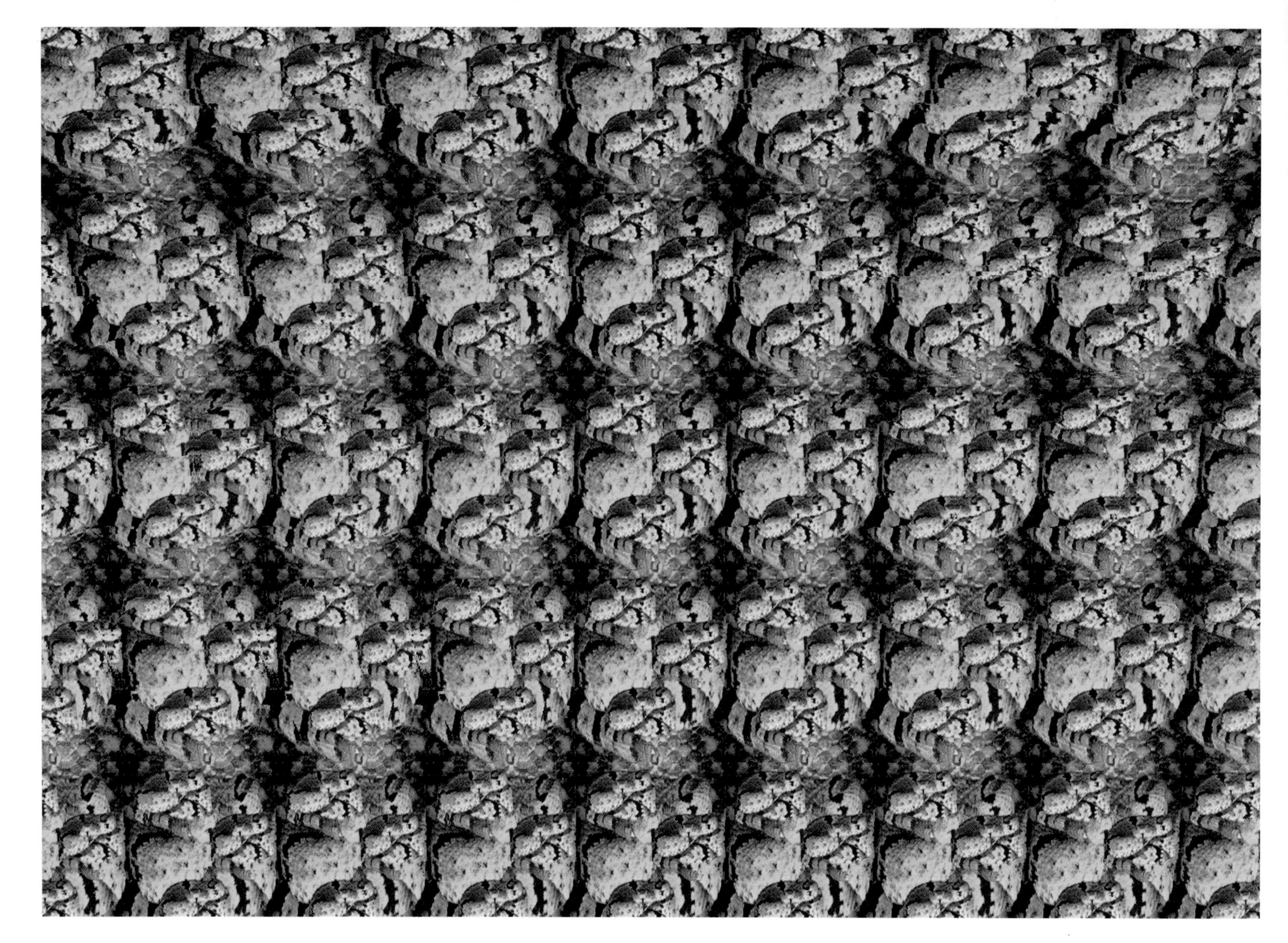

READY TO STRIKE

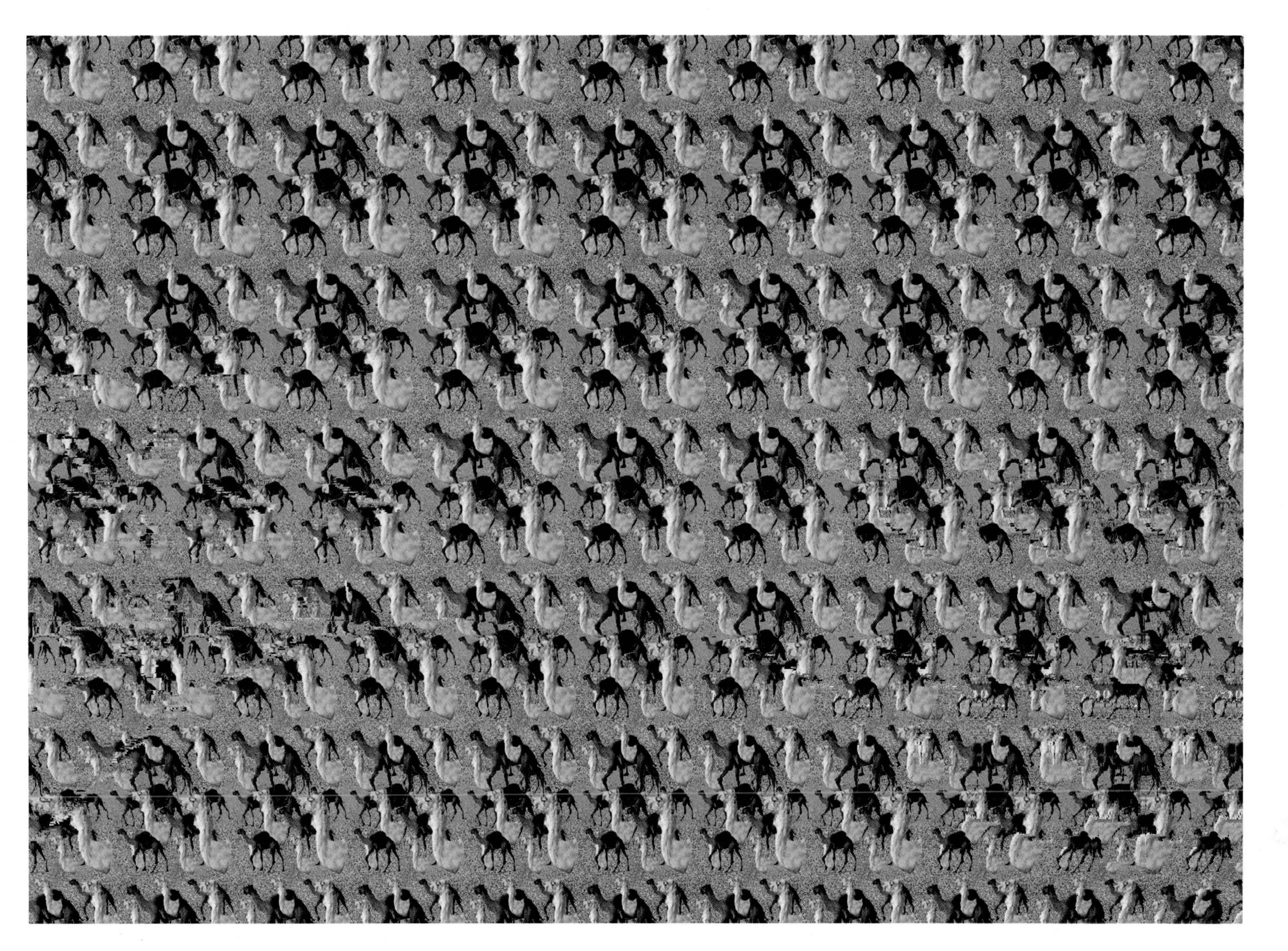

WANDERING THE DESERT

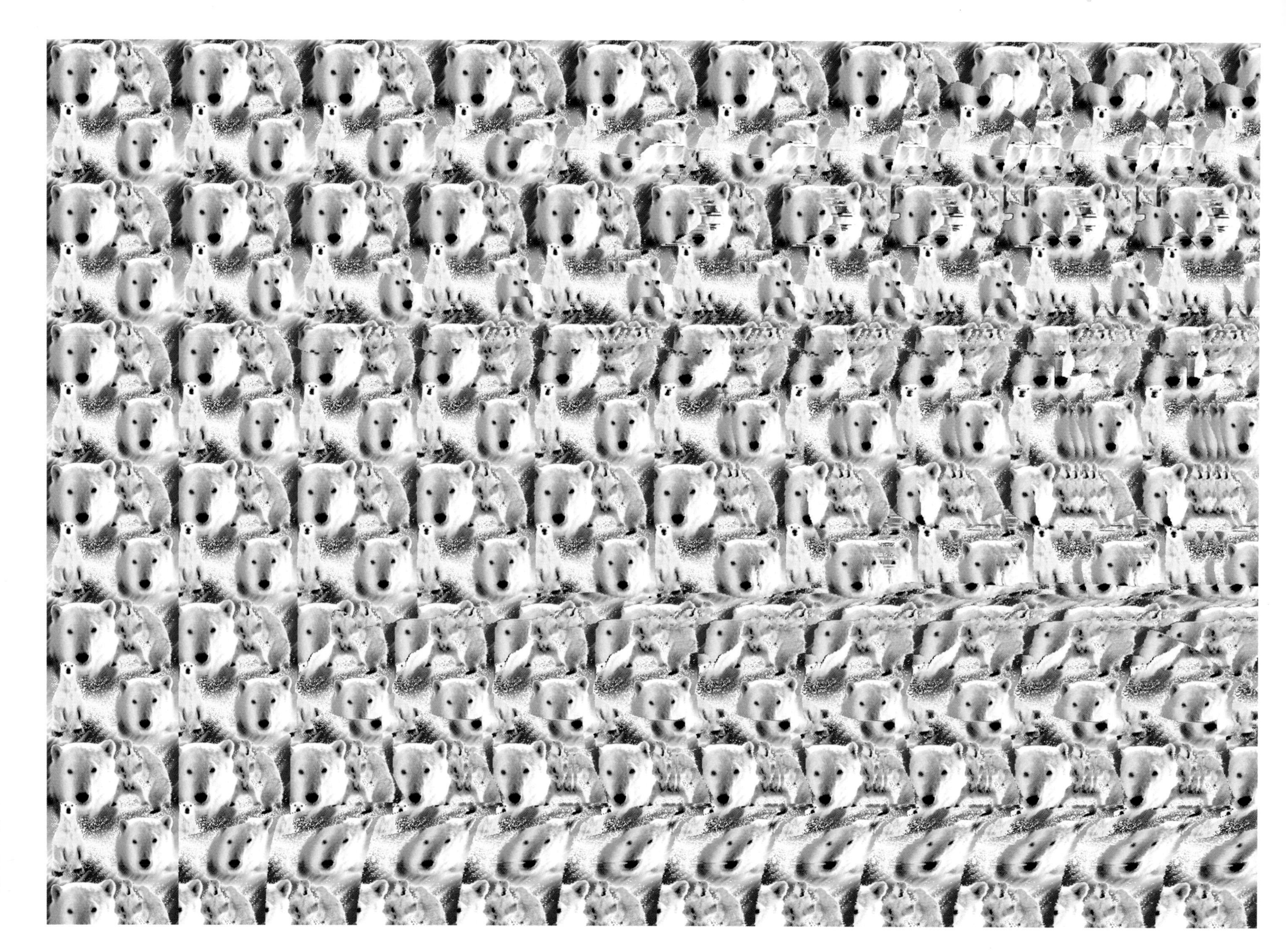

POLAR BEARS

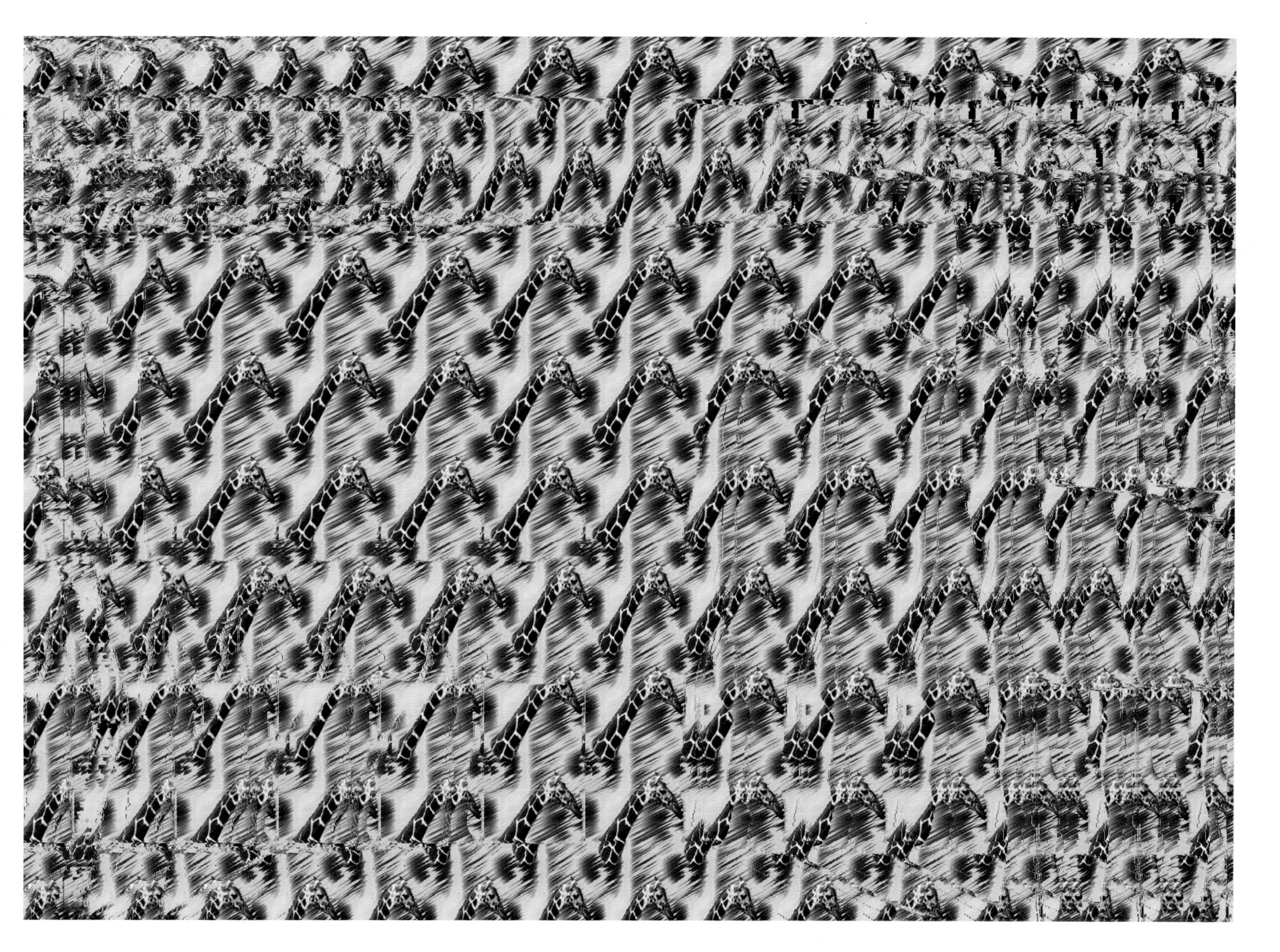

LUNCHTIME

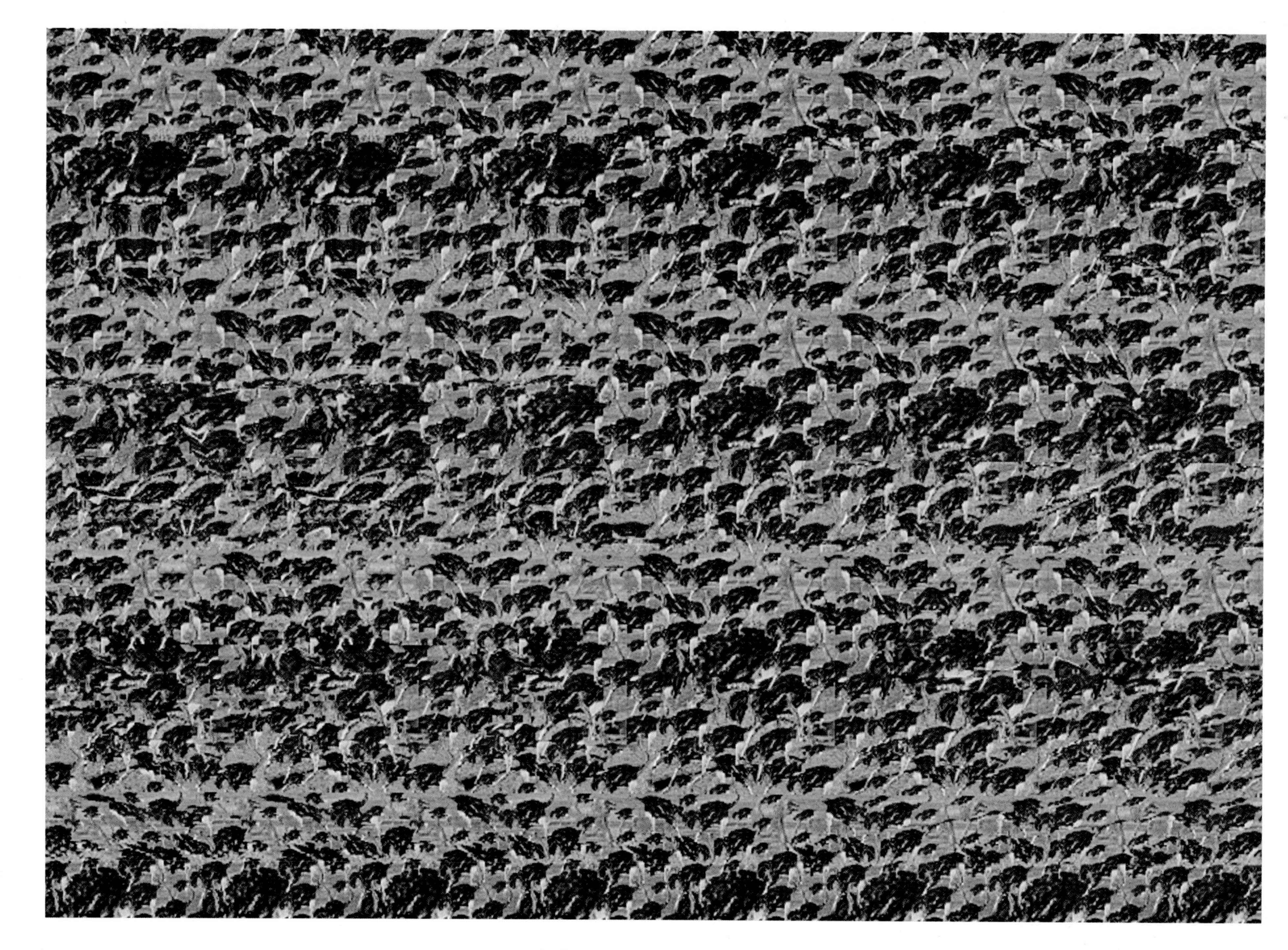

OSTRICH RACE

SEA TURTLES

ON THE PROWL

CHEETAH LOUNGE

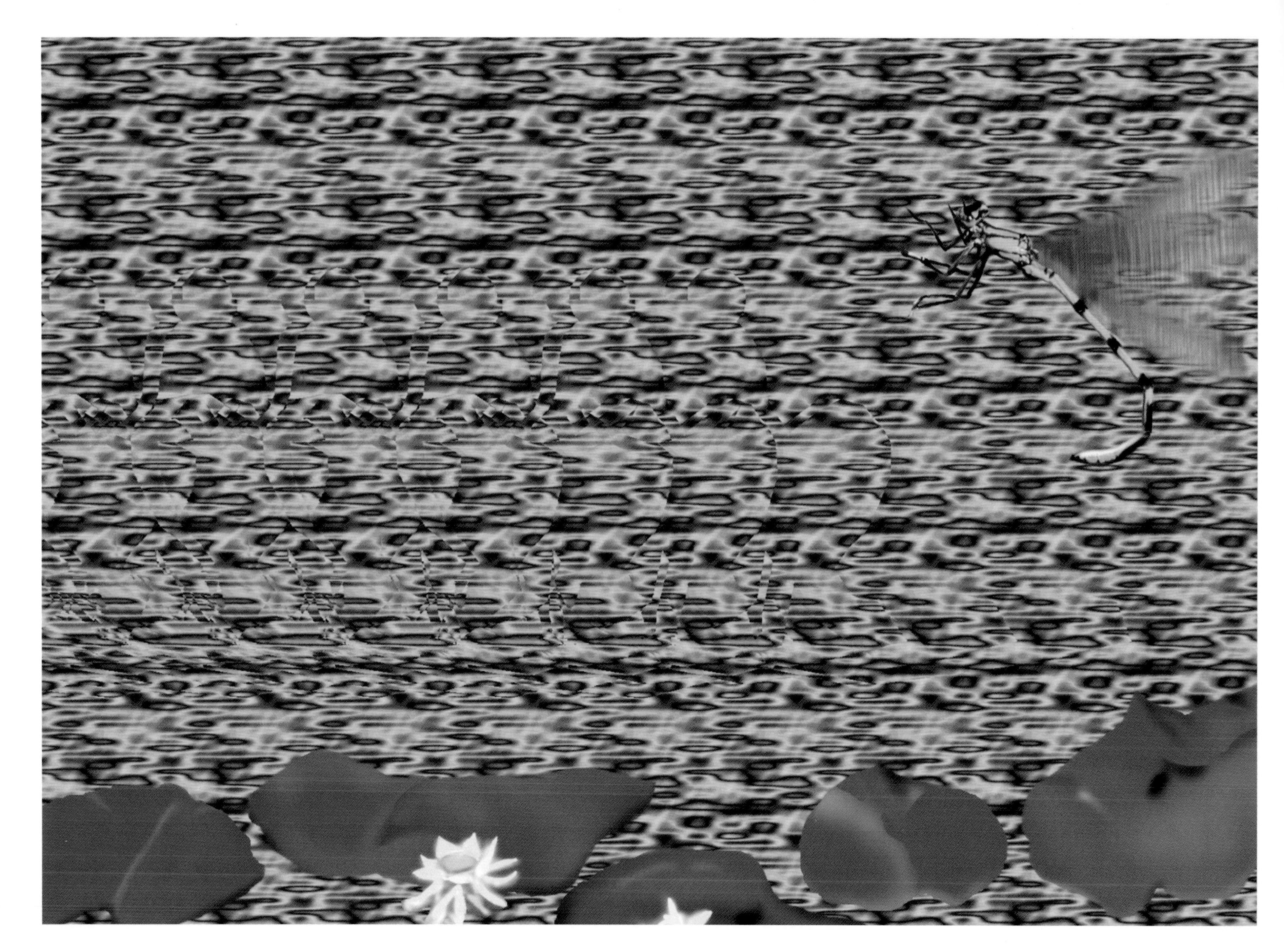

LEAPING LILY PADS

HAPPY HIPPOS

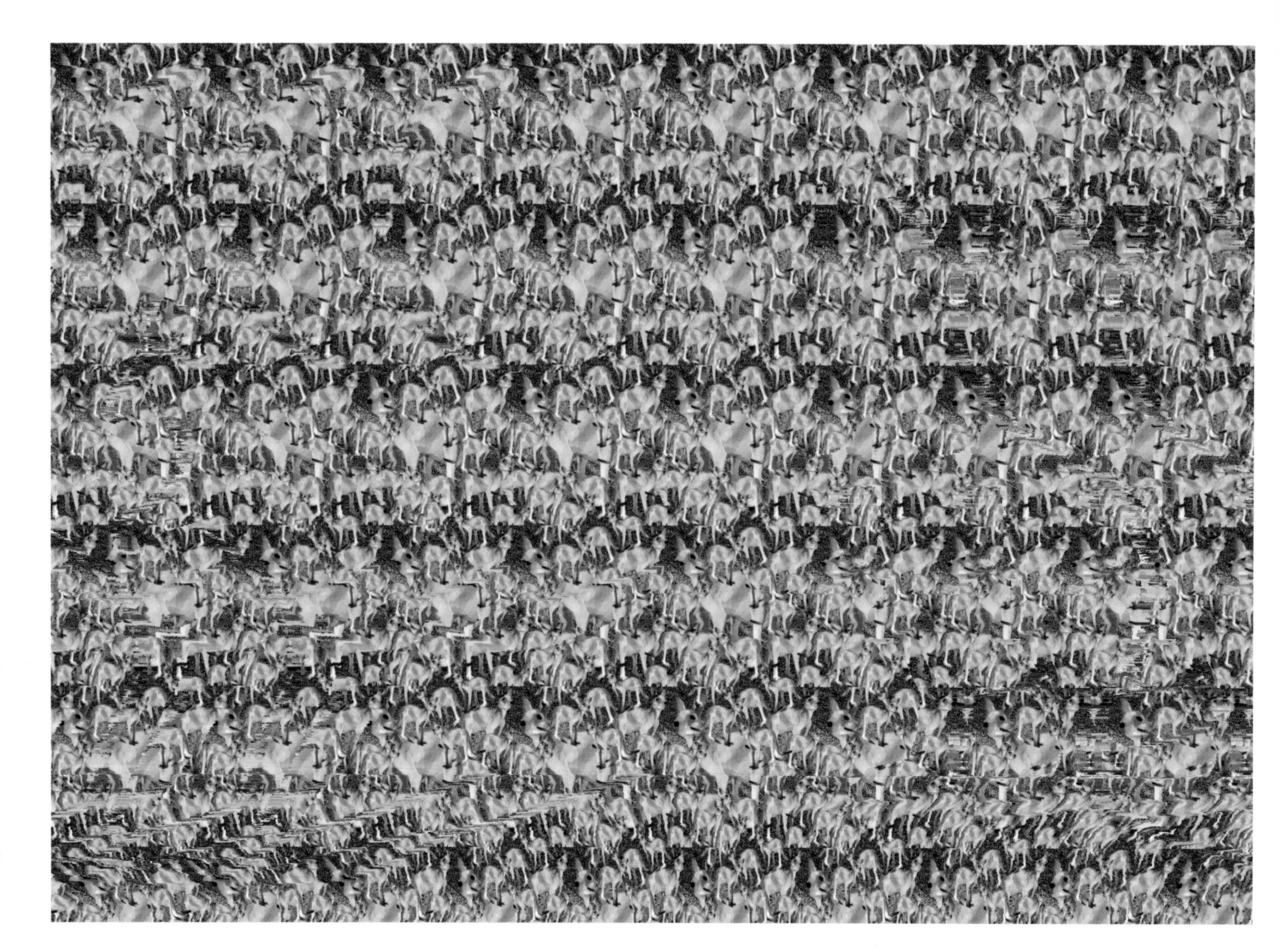

HOPPING AROUND

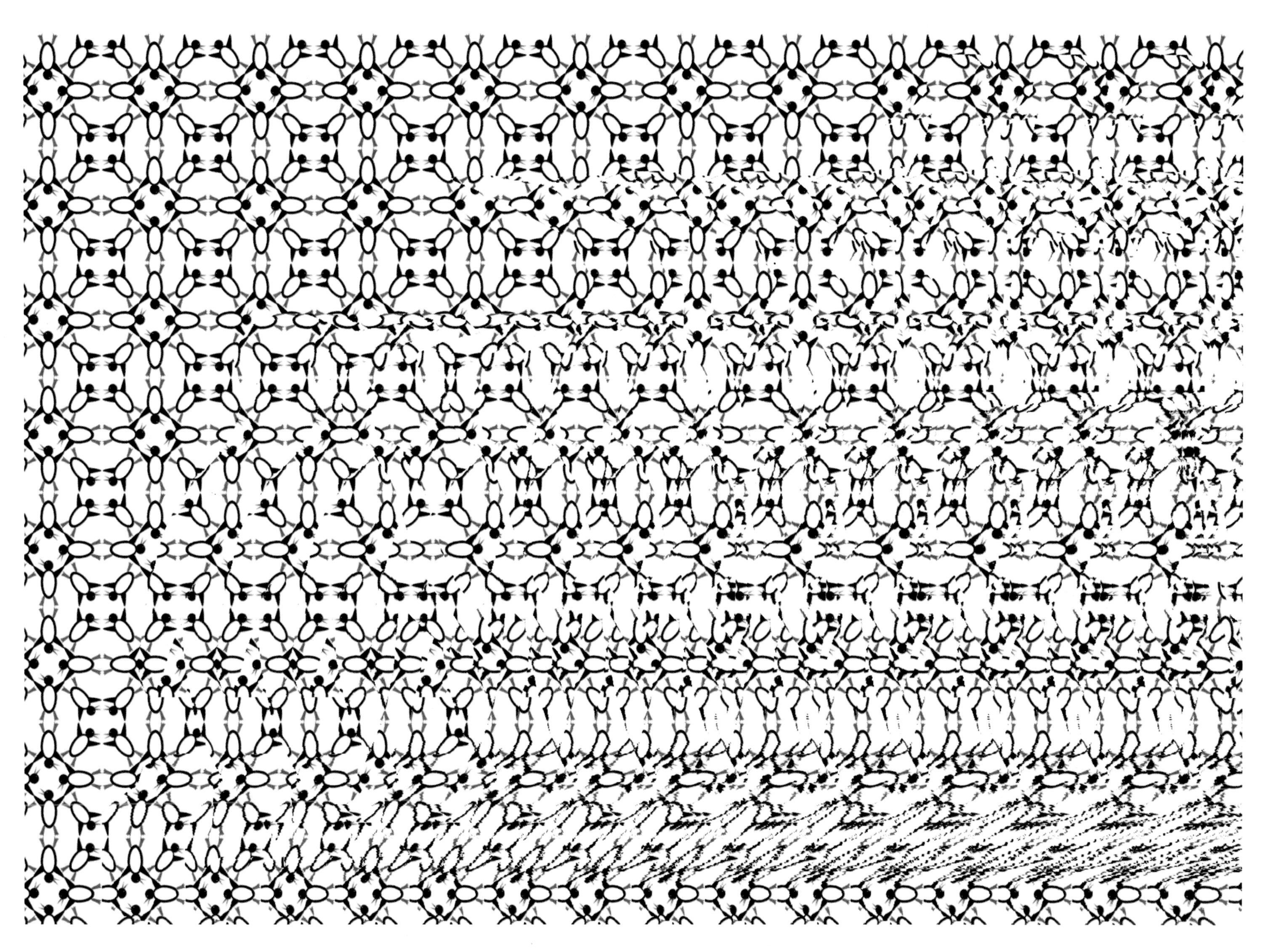

PENGUINS

ULTRA 3-D *Magic* HIDDEN IMAGES

JUNGLE KING

1

CHARGE!!

2

FLYING HOME

3

BAT CAVE

4

BIRDS OF A FEATHER

5

JUMPING THE GATE

6

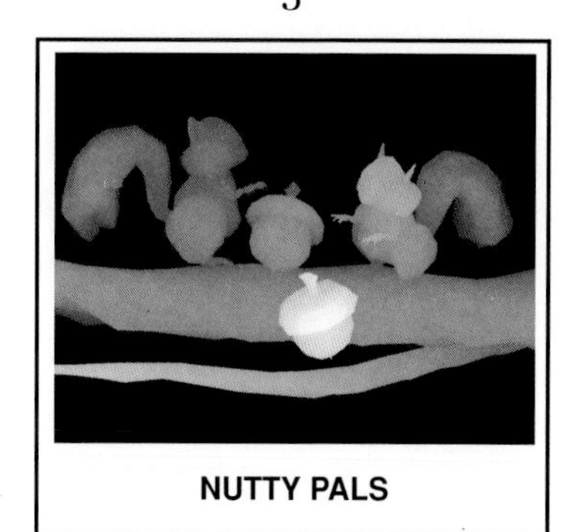
NUTTY PALS

7

ZEBRA COUNTRY

8

ELEPHANTS

9

MONKEYING AROUND

10

MASTERS OF THE MOUNTAINTOPS

11

RABBIT SEASON

12

LAIR OF THE WHITE WOLF

13

ULTRA 3-D Magic HIDDEN IMAGES

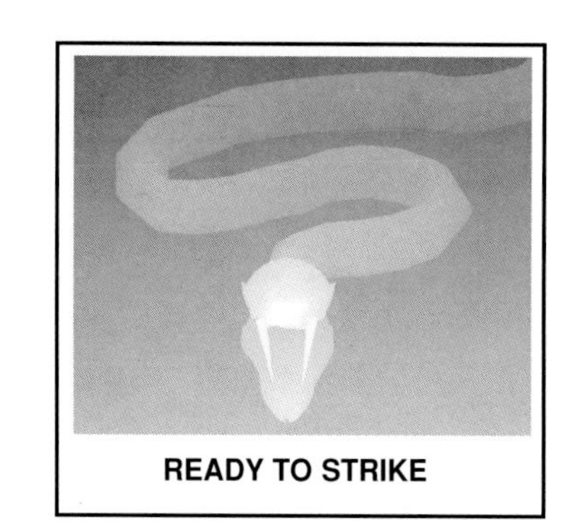
READY TO STRIKE
14

WANDERING THE DESERT
15

POLAR BEARS
16

LUNCHTIME
17

OSTRICH RACE
18

SEA TURTLES
19

ON THE PROWL
20

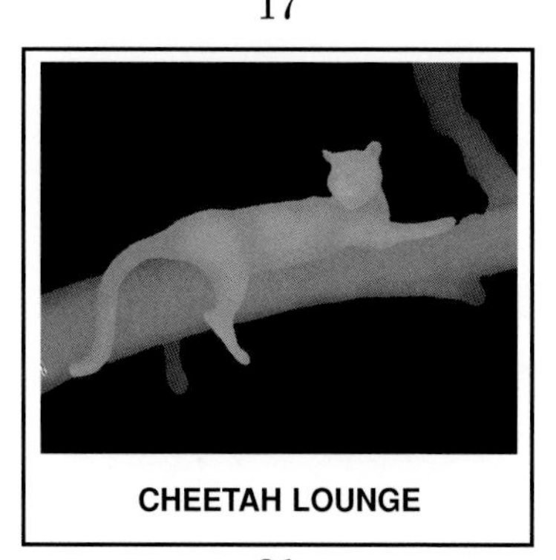
CHEETAH LOUNGE
21

LEAPING LILY PADS
22

HAPPY HIPPOS
23

HOPPING AROUND
24

PENGUINS
25

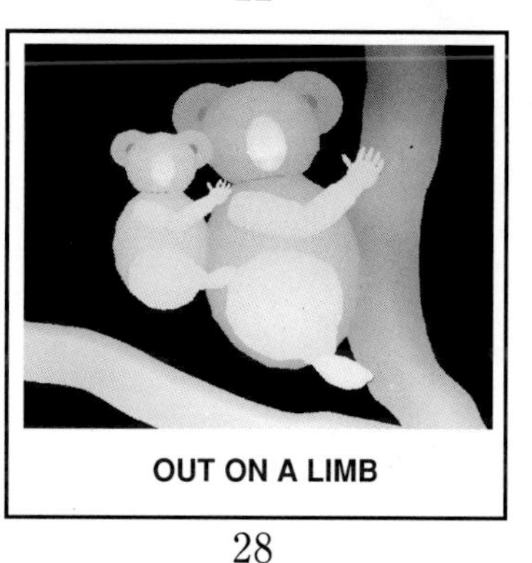
OUT ON A LIMB
28

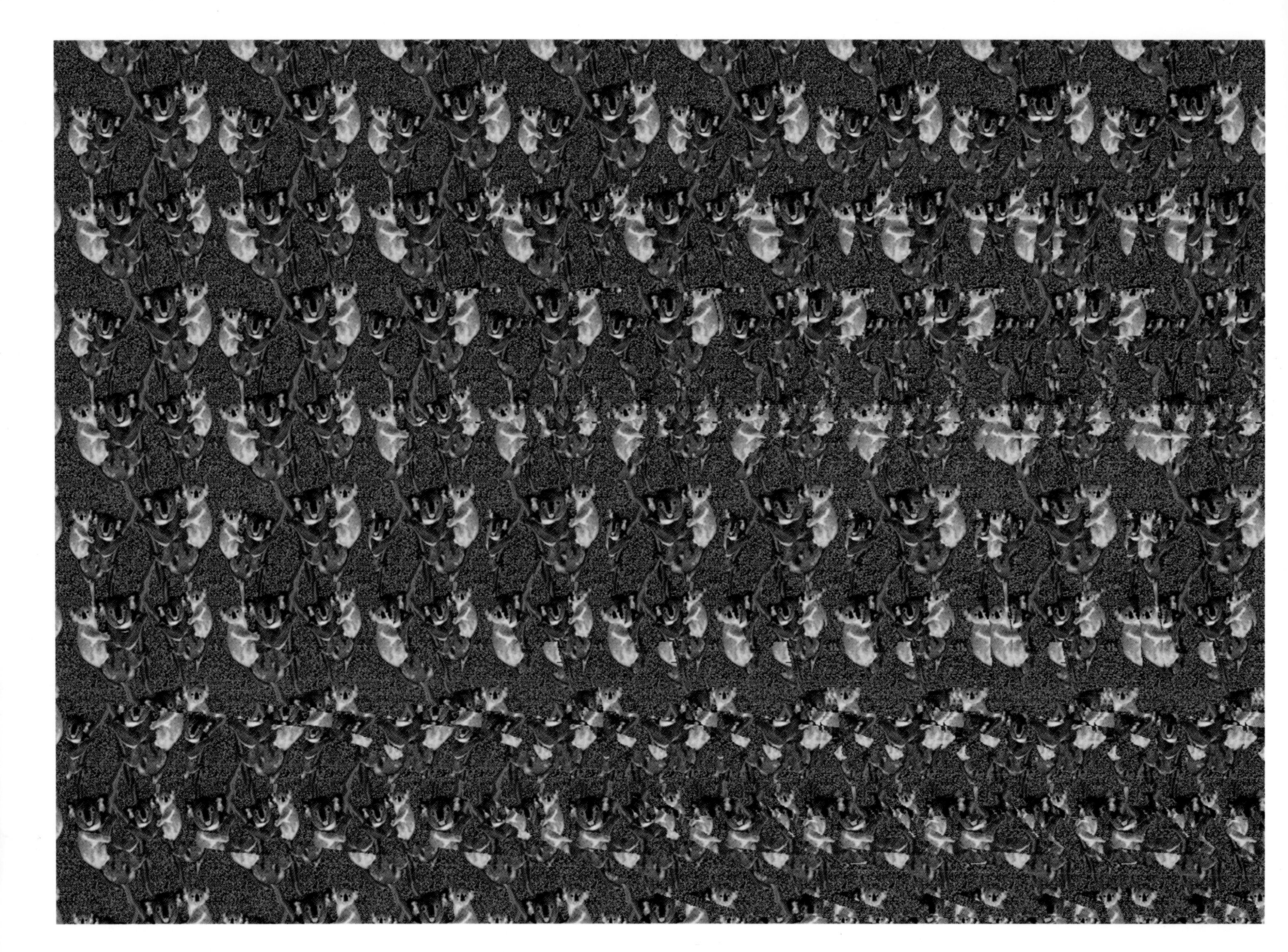

OUT ON A LIMB